A War of Two Halves

Written by

Tim Barrow and Paul Beeson

Dramaturgy by

Bruce Strachan

This first edition published and copyright 2022
by Tippermuir Books Ltd, Perth, Scotland.
mail@tippermuirbooks.co.uk www.tippermuirbooks.co.uk.

ISBN 978-1-913836-15-3 (paperback)

A CIP catalogue record for this book is available from the British Library.

Editorial and Project coordination by Dr Paul S Philippou.

Cover design by Matthew Mackie.
Editorial support: Steve Zajda.
Text design, layout, and artwork by Bernard Chandler [graffik].
Text set in Interstate Light 9/11.5pt with Bold titling.

Printed and bound by Ashford Colour Press Ltd, Gosport, PO13 OFW,

Dedicated to the players,
coaches and management of
Heart of Midlothian Football Club,
Season 1914-15

A WAR OF TWO HALVES

CAST

(In order of appearance)

THE ANGEL

ALFIE BRIGGS

JOHN McCARTNEY

PATRICK CROSSAN

HARRY WATTIE

DUNCAN CURRIE

ANNAN NESS

ERNIE ELLIS

SIR GEORGE McCRAE

JOHN LEONARD

A WAR OF TWO HALVES

'We are greatly honoured to be returning to Tynecastle Park with this iconic story that is absolutely synonymous with Edinburgh and Heart of Midlothian Football Club. With November 2018 marking 100 years since the signing of the Armistice, it is a poignant time to share the remarkable story of "the bravest team". Hearts fans will have heard of McCrae's Battalion – this is another chance to really understand their story. For a wider audience, the opportunity to experience a behind-the-scenes view of a football stadium in a dramatic retelling of historical events will be a truly unique theatre experience.'

Bruce Strachan, *Director*

'It is absolutely fitting that in the year of the centenary of the Armistice, Tynecastle Park should host This is My Story's production, *A War of Two Halves*. By telling the story that started with a rallying cry at our ground from Lieutenant-Col. Sir George McCrae, it pays homage to the footballers who volunteered to go to the front in 1914. Many paid the ultimate price for their country. Their memory will never be forgotten and is honoured throughout Tynecastle Park. This is a story that needs to be told to as broad an audience as possible. It takes on particular poignancy as it comes to life in the very ground the team left in 1914, with action taking place throughout the stadium. This unique "promenade performance" will undoubtedly be a standout piece in this year's Fringe Festival and we would urge parents to consider bringing their children to experience this historically important production and to learn of the sacrifice of "the bravest team".' [2018]

Lianne Parry, *Head of Heritage,*
Heart of Midlothian Football Club

'The timing of Bruce Strachan's direction and the technical execution is evocative and perfectly pitched, while the group of actors blend testosterone-fuelled action and the sensitivity of scared young men in their performances.'

The Scotsman

'There are so many moments in this play that are theatrical genius. In particular, at the heart of the play, I loved when they changed from football kit to uniform and took us to the trenches, it's beautifully staged, director Bruce Strachan has done an outstanding job. We all know how this ends, and the final scene takes place in the memorial garden, where each actor pays tribute to their real-life counterpart. This is so moving, so respectful, and every single audience member was affected.'

Paul T Davies, *britishtheatre.com*

'The thought that has gone into this piece of theatre, beyond performance and venue, deserves every ounce of respect we can muster. *A War of Two Halves* is a stunning piece of writing, with a sentimental heart of reverence.'

corrblimey.blog

'Written by Paul Beeson & Tim Barrow, and featuring a castof talented young Scottish actors, *A War of Two Halves*, directed by Bruce Strachan, is an evocative and dramatic journey through Tynecastle Park led by the players/soldiers in a unique site-specific performance. The performance of *A War of Two Halves* last year was one of the most emotional I have seen...this remarkable story will bring a lump to the throat of anyon e, no matter what team you support – and even if you have no interest in football. A supremely talented cast ensures there will be no more powerful performances at the Edinburgh Fringe than this one.'

Mike Smith, *The Edinburgh Reporter*

'Devastating emotion...The sincerity, emotional directness, and beautiful staging of *A War Of Two Halves* deserves to transcend sporting allegiances.'

AllEdinburghTheatre.com

ORIGINAL CAST AND PRODUCTION TEAM

Tynecastle Park, 2-19 August 2018

Alfie Briggs	Paul Beeson/Bryan Lowe
Patrick Crossan	John Cairns
Duncan Currie	Fraser Bryson
Ernie Ellis	Mark Rannoch
John Leonard	Tim Barrow
John McCartney	Tim Barrow
Sir George McCrae	Bryan Lowe/Paul Beeson
Annan Ness	Tony McGeever
The Angel	Elspeth Turner
Harry Wattie	Terence Rae
Director	Bruce Strachan
Associate Producer	Simon Beattie
Writers	Tim Barrow and Paul Beeson
Musical Director	Matthew Brown
Set Design	Eve Murray
Sound Design	Philip Pinsky
Costume Design	Natasha Murray
Props Assistant	Emily Ingram
Carpenter	Charlie McIntyre

The following people/organisations were involved in supporting the production:

A big-hearted thank you goes to Lianne Parry, Ann Park, Hattie Chandler, the club historian David Speed, the museum staff and all the brilliant people at Heart of Midlothian Football Club for accommodating us. Many other people/organisations were involved in supporting the production and all require our thanks and gratitude: Jack Alexander for his incredible work, the McCrae's Battalion Trust, Jo Barrow and The Edinburgh Makars, Queen Margaret University, The History Bunker, David McFarlane, Symon Macintyre, Kim Bergsagei, Kieran Topping, Lesley Johnston, Thomas Morgan, Ian Cunningham, the National Theatre of Scotland, the amazing Simon Beattie, and Nathan Scott Dunn who had another Fringe play to star in.

This Is My Story Productions was formed in 2017 to stage *A War of Two Halves*, which played to rave reviews and fantastic audience acclaim at Tynecastle Park as part of the Edinburgh Fringe in 2018 and 2019.

Nonsense Room Productions was established in 2002.
Its previous shows at the Edinburgh Fringe include:
The Ballad of James II by Douglas Maxwell, *A Midsummer Night's Dream*, *Romeo and Juliet*, *The Apprentice* by Simon Beattie and *Handling Bach* by Paul Barz, all performed at the iconic Rosslyn Chapel. Its work for young people includes: *Hairy Maclary & Friends*, *Shark in the Park*, *You Choose* and *Little Red Riding Hood*.

In 2011, *Hairy Maclary & Friends* was invited to play at Sydney Opera House, Australia, for its Christmas season. Since then it has been invited to take part in the acclaimed Kidsfest in both Hong Kong and Singapore, and has toured extensively in the UK, Ireland, Australia and New Zealand.

www.thisismystoryproductions.co.uk

ALSO AVAILABLE

Sweet F.A. 1916. The men fight on the Western Front. The women work in the factories, and form football teams, playing other factory teams across Scotland and raising money for the war effort. Women's football fast becomes the most popular game in the land. Fearful that the men's game is being eclipsed, the football authorities ban the women's game in 1921. Inspired by true events, *Sweet F.A.* tells the vibrant story of one women's factory football team from Fountainbridge, Edinburgh, their friendships, loves, losses and battles with their fierce rivals from Leith.

Blending history, humour, passion and poignancy with live music and song, *Sweet F.A.* dramatises the little known truth about what happened to the women's game. It premiered to great review at the 2021 Edinburgh Festival Fringe.

ABOUT THE AUTHORS

Tim Barrow is the co-writer of *A War Of Two Halves*. He trained as an actor at Drama Centre London, graduating with a BA Hons in 2001. His debut play, *Guy*, played at London's Pleasance Theatre, directed by Michael Fentiman. *Union* premiered at Edinburgh's Lyceum Theatre, directed by Mark Thomson, and is published by Playdead Press. *Neither God Nor Angel* played at Oran Mor/Traverse, directed by Ryan Alexander Dewar. Tim was one of five writers who created *The Sunnyside Centre* for Village Pub Theatre, directed by Caitlin Skinner. *A War Of Two Halves*, co-written with Paul Beeson, played at Tynecastle Park in 2018 and 2019. Tim founded Lyre Productions to make independent Scottish feature films, writing and producing the award-winning indie Scottish road movie *The Inheritance*, Edinburgh love story *The Space Between*, and schizophrenia love story road movie *Riptide* - currently screening at film festivals worldwide.

Paul Beeson is the co-writer of *A War Of Two Halves.* He is an Edinburgh-born actor, writer, teacher and co-founder of This Is My Story Productions. He has many theatre credits and has previously toured the UK and internationally with acclaimed company Nonsense Room Productions, performing in shows including *Shark in the Park, You Choose* and *Ae Fond Kiss.* Paul's first venture into writing was sketch show *A Beginner's Guide to the Fringe* in 2005 after which he co-wrote and performed in the critically successful Edinburgh Fringe sell-out production *A War of Two Halves* in 2018 and 2019. The play received 5-star reviews and was one of britishtheatre.com's Critics Choices of 2019. He has also co-written three short films: *The Hardest Hobbit to Break, Route de Sort* and *Last Night in the Cockpit.* He is currently developing two comedy drama series, *The VHS Diaries* and *Theatre in Education*, and has also recently filmed a pilot for Scottish sitcom *Game of Cones* and recorded an audio drama called *From An Island.*

Bruce Strachan is the director of *A War Of Two Halves.* He trained at the Royal Scottish Academy of Music and Drama (now RCS). He works as an acting teacher, director and producer, and is currently a lecturer in acting at Queen Margaret University, Edinburgh. He has worked throughout the UK for companies including Hull Truck, TAG Theatre Glasgow, The Arches, The National Youth Theatre of Great Britain and the National Theatre of Scotland. Bruce has been artistic director of Nonsense Room Productions since 2002 and has directed many shows including *Shark in the Park, You Choose* as well as *Hairy Maclary & Friends* in both the UK and internationally – including a summer season at Sydney Opera House. For This Is My Story Productions, he has also directed *Sweet F.A.*

DIRECTOR'S NOTE

This play was originally written to be a promenade performance at Tynecastle Park, home of Heart of Midlothian since 1886. The piece was developed, with kind permission from the football club, to reflect the journey of the players from that very football field to the fields of the Somme. In our version, it travels from the supporters' bar, to the stands, visits the home dressing-room and concludes in the beautiful memorial garden in the far corner of the ground. The correlation between the scenes and the locations adds huge power to the drama. Being outside for the trenches section is also particularly powerful.

The play could, of course, be performed in a traditional theatre with an appropriate set or indeed in another stadium or perhaps a football field - as creators we are open to creative ways to tell the story.

It is vital, however, that the reverence with which these men and this story is held by the football clubs who contributed to McCrae's Battalion - Hearts, Hibernian, Dunfermline, Raith Rovers and East Fife - is respected at all times. In addition, there are living relatives of those depicted and consequently, it is critical that the story of the 'real' Heart of Midlothian players is not altered in any significant way without our prior engagement.

It may be possible to be more creative with 'The Angel' character or indeed elements of the music. The lament that is played has been chosen by the individual fiddle performer involved in the production; it is a crucial element to underpin key moments in the play. The original piece was 'Flight of the Eaglets' ('Lady MacRoberts McCrae's' Lament') - formerly for bagpipe and played on fiddle. Also crucial is the 'Geordie McCrae' song, which is used in various arrangements throughout the play. It is an evocative rallying cry key to the moment when the men prepare to go over the top. Other elements, however, such as scene changes are open to interpretation.

John Leonard is a fictitious character. His inclusion, nonetheless, is vital to acknowledge the players from other clubs in McCrae's Battalion and those supporters who joined up to follow the players.

For any performance queries - please do get in touch via: thisismystoryproductions@gmail.com.

This play is based on true events and depicts real people but some elements have been dramatised. Whilst we strive for accuracy and authenticity, we acknowledge any mistakes as ours.

FOREWORD

The story of the players from Heart of Midlothian Football Club who volunteered, en masse, to fight for McCrae's Battalion (16th Battalion Royal Scots) in the First World War, will forever be woven into the fabric of the history of that football club.

Writing and producing this play, and having been able to perform it at Tynecastle Park as lifelong Hearts fans, has been the greatest honour and privilege.

In telling the story of the pals of the sporting battalion, we are entirely mindful that it is a real story, about people with living relatives. We strove throughout the process to honour their memory and respect their legacy, whilst trying to tell the world their remarkable tale - always in the knowledge that we were standing on the shoulders of giants. As theatre makers, the drama of this story is extraordinarily powerful. It is the very definition of a tragedy.

In bringing the piece to life, we must acknowledge the work of Jack Alexander and his book, *McCrae's Battalion* (2003). We also must thank David Speed, the official club historian, and the team at The Heart of Midlothian Museum for their insight and input.

Furthermore, we are especially grateful to all the staff at Heart of Midlothian who have welcomed us so warmly and generously to Tynecastle Park. We must give particular mention to Lianne Parry and Ann Park, who were unequivocal in their support for the show. Without them, there would be no play of which to speak.

It is hard to pinpoint the exact origin of the play - it rather came about through a series of small events that eventually led to production. Tim gave me a copy of McCrae's Battalion in 2004 as a gift. We have a shared interest in the Great War, and football of course, having sat together in high school history classes; and have been friends since primary school. When I read the book, I knew instantly that it was a story I would love to tell as a piece of theatre, given the inherent drama within it. I did not, however, do much with the idea at that time.

Fast forward to 2017, when Paul and I were watching an Edinburgh Fringe show and, over a pint or two, got talking about what we could potentially do in 2018. We had sat together for several years as season ticket holders in Section G of the Wheatfield Stand during the early 2000s. During that particular conversation we discovered we both had an idea for a play about McCrae's and the Hearts players. We shared our idea with Tim, who soon came on board and we began sketching out ideas for what the show could be.

Paul in particular did a power of research and slowly but surely, draft by draft and meeting by meeting, the story began to come together. We were always keen to perform it at Tynecastle and for it to be a promenade piece of sorts depending on how much of the stadium we were able to use. Through the club's generosity, we were given fantastic access, including to the Home dressing room, and we were able to write the story to match the route we take through the ground.

The show was brilliantly supported by the design work of Eve Murray, Natasha Murray, and Philip Pinsky all of whom did a terrific job adding to the tone, look and sound of the piece. Simon Beattie and Matthew Brown of Nonsense Room Productions also contributed significantly to the production, and we are very thankful for their support in helping us to produce the piece.

Finally, we must pay tribute to all of the performers who have joined us in performing this show. It was at times the most punishing of schedules and our own battalion spirit was needed to get us through four show days when each featured pouring rain - despite how atmospheric this made it. They always approached it with good humour and a determination to do justice to this incredible story. We are extremely thankful to them for bringing this story to life with such passion.

Bruce Strachan, October 2021

ACT ONE

Home, 1 July 1933

The sitting room of Alfie Briggs.

The Angel enters and plays 'The Hearts Song' on her fiddle. As the music rises, Briggs hurriedly enters through the door and shuts it quickly. The Angel abruptly stops playing and moves to the edge of the space. Briggs locks the door and stands for a moment. Silence. There is a knock at the door, which shakes Briggs out of himself. It is his wife, Alice, voiced by The Angel.

Alice Alfie? Alfie! Are you alright love? Alfie, talk tae me...

Briggs I'm alright. I just need tae be alone... for a while.

Alice Can I get you anything? Do you want a cup of tea?

Briggs No, I'm fine.

Alice Just a half-cup?

Briggs No! [*Composing himself*] No, thank you.

Beat

Alice I'll put the kettle on.

Briggs goes to the bookcase and picks up an old wooden box. As he does, The Angel appears, playing a lament on her fiddle. She is part of the action and the audience, drifting as it suits her. Briggs sits in his armchair and opens the box. He takes out his old Scotland jersey and puts it on over his shirt. He takes out his old Heart of Midlothian jersey, which he holds up before placing on the table. He takes out a 1914-15 team photograph and does the same. Lastly, he brings out a bullet, which he inspects. He is on the verge of tears, when there is another knock at the door. The lament stops suddenly.

Alice Alfie, there's a cup of tea oot here for you. Don't let it go cold.

Briggs Thanks hen.

Alice Please don't stay locked in there too long, eh.

Beat

Despite the door being locked, it opens and John McCartney walks in. He is smartly dressed and carries the cup of tea. Briggs is surprised to see him.

Briggs Boss? What are you doing here?

McCartney Here's your tea.

Briggs But you're...

McCartney Don't let it get cold.

Briggs takes the cup of tea.

Briggs Thank you.

Beat

Briggs I was at your funeral...

McCartney [*Looking at the photograph*] Some team, eh? Could have won the League.

Briggs Should have.

McCartney [*Picking up the bullet*] Is this the bullet with your name on it?

Briggs No. There's two of those still lodged in my back.

McCartney Your playing days are over then?

Briggs [*Half smiling*] You could say that...

McCartney You were a fine half-back. Shame only half your back's working now. No offence.

Briggs [*Laughing*] None taken, Boss.

Beat

McCartney First of July. It's that time of year again.

Briggs Aye.

McCartney When you need to be alone.

Briggs Aye.

McCartney Then why am I here?

Briggs Dunno. [*Considers the question*] Maybe I'm ready to talk. See...Alice doesnae understand. Most folk dinnae understand. You do. I ken you werenae there, but you do...mair than most.

McCartney What about Ness? And Crossan?

Briggs I still see them. At Paddy's Bar.

McCartney Thick as thieves you lot were.

Briggs We still are, Boss...but it's different...you're a comfort, I suppose.

McCartney Am I now? Isn't that lovely! It wasn't like that when we first met.

It is 1912, in the dressing room at Tynecastle after the Scotland v Wales Junior International. Briggs is younger, more spritely. McCartney is much the same. The Angel plays a reel.

McCartney Alfie Briggs? John McCartney. I'm the manager of Heart of Midlothian.

Briggs I know who you are Mr McCartney. It's a pleasure, sir!

They shake hands. McCartney doesn't let go and the handshake continues through the following dialogue.

McCartney You had a fine game today. Incredibly composed. Very impressive for your first International.

Briggs Thank you, sir.

McCartney Remind me...Who do you play for?

Briggs Scotland.

McCartney Your club team, son.

Briggs Oh...Clydebank Juniors, sir.

McCartney I'd like you to play for me.

Briggs ...

McCartney How would you like to play for the Hearts?

Briggs Ah...Well, that sounds...I'd...

McCartney I'd very much like you to sign for us.

Briggs I'll need to talk to...

McCartney Allow me to blunt, Mr Briggs. I have locked the dressing room door and I won't let you leave until we shake hands on a contract.

Briggs We're already shaking hands...

McCartney Wonderful! [*The handshake ends abruptly. McCartney picks up the Hearts jersey from the armchair and hands it to Briggs.*] Then it's settled!

We are back in 1933.

Briggs Like I said. You're a comfort. A ghost from the past I dinnae mind seeing. I dinnae mind you popping in. Like the rest of the boys...[*Pointing to his own head*] there's room in here for them an' all.

McCartney Aye. Just big enough for a reunion. Speaking of which...

McCartney nods to the door.

Briggs Aye. We'll catch you up, Boss.

McCartney Don't take too long, Alfie. We can't start without you.

McCartney pats Briggs on the shoulder and leaves through the locked door. Alfie watches him leave, then removes his Scotland jersey. He turns to face the audience and addresses them directly.

Briggs I'm no' like this all the time, you know! I dinnae usually lock mysel' in my living room and talk to ghosts. It's just...it's the first of July. But I think of the good times too. Oh, aye! There were good times! I've kept quiet about it for a long while. But now I'm ready. Let me tell you a story about the finest group of lads I've ever known. The sacrifice and bravery of these lads cannae be allowed to fade. I want to give my pals a voice. And for their voice to be heard, I need you.

Briggs jumps up from his chair. He is younger once more. The Angel begins to play a jauntier tune.

Briggs I'm going to take you back to the Front. This is our story!

Briggs beckons the audience to follow him. He and The Angel lead them into the new Main Stand. The Angel continues playing during the journey.

Briggs I'm sure I dinnae have to introduce the old girl to anyone here, but I am a great believer in formalities! This is Tynecastle! Home of the Hearts! Breathe in that malt-filled air! What do you think of the new stand? It's no' long been finished. This is a feat of engineering, one of the best modern stands in Scotland. The rising public demand necessitated the construction. The country's most notable stadium architect was commissioned to design this... Archibald Leitch. He had already been commissioned to design Ibrox, Anfield, Goodison Park, Stamford Bridge, Villa Park, White Hart Lane... the list goes on. Esteemed company indeed. When it was completed in the October, it was the most advanced in Scotland. It went over budget a wee bit...awright, it trebled in cost! We had to sell Percy Dawson to Blackburn Rovers for a British record transfer fee of... wait for it... two point five... thousand pounds! Serious money! Aye, it's some sight, running oot on the park to see this stand full to the rafters... the adulation, the passion... and the noise! A roaring sea of maroon! It wasn't quite finished in time for the start of the season, but it was partially opened just in time for Celtic's visit on the fifteenth of August 1914.

The following commentary is heard. Briggs watches the empty pitch and reacts as if he is at the game, cheering and shouting.

Commentator *Welcome to Tynecastle on a sunny, blustery day that marks the opening day of the 1914/15 season, where the Heart of Midlothian welcome the strongly-fancied Celtic team. Over 18,000 spectators are in attendance. The Celtic fans do their best to be heard, but are drowned out by the enthusiastic Hearts supporters. The referee blows his whistle, and the Hearts kick off, playing towards the Gorgie Road end. They are immediately pressed by the Parkhead side, most observers' tip for this season's title.*

The Celtic attack strongly, repelled by an adamant defence led by Archie Boyd. Strong tackling by the full-back Paddy Crossan, there. And there's Mercer, the centre-half, the rock of this team, galvanising his Hearts players. A fine block! Oh but he's injured himself. Bravely he's carrying on.

Second half continues in the pattern of the first. Wattie is playing his usual robust, sound game. Chance here - the ball falls to him - he's scored! Excellent strike! One-nil to the Heart of Midlothian! The Celtic look stunned.

Speedie and Wilson combine nicely on the left wing for Hearts, as they have all game. Another chance - and Gracie scores. Two-nil! The fans of the Heart of Midlothian are singing lustily!

The full-time whistle blows and the Hearts have defeated the reigning champions Celtic. Only by an exceptional exhibition of pluck, grit and determination has this victory been obtained by the Tynecastle brigade! An excellent start to their season.

Briggs Final score... Heart of Midlothian two, Celtic nil!

The Angel [*Reading from a newspaper*] 'Crowds of callous, thoughtless fools gather in their thousands to watch the awful farce of football. Has the country gone stark mad? Is the flag under whose folds we enjoy glorious British freedom of less importance now than a League flag, or some other footballing trophy? *The Scotsman.*'

Briggs Twenty-sixth of August 1914. Over 4,000 spectators witnessed the final of the Dunedin Cup competition between the Heart of Midlothian and the Hibernians at Tynecastle last night. From the start the Hibernians were hopelessly outclassed. The Hearts scored three goals within fifteen minutes of the kick-off, Gracie, Graham and Malcolm being the successful marksmen. This lead they maintained until the interval, and after half an hours' play in the second half the Hearts put in another three goals, Graham, Speedie and Gracie scoring in quick succession. Final score... Heart of Midlothian six goals, Hibernians nil. Some result eh! It's not quite as good as our record of ten-two, but it's no bad! We were off to a flyer at the start of the season. Next up, were the Rangers at Ibrox.

Commentator *Welcome to Ibrox Park where the Rangers welcome the formidable Heart of Midlothian. Despite the miserable Glasgow weather, and the absence of many football followers who have enlisted in the army, a splendid crowd of 30,000 is in attendance, the biggest of the season.*

The referee, Mr Murray of Stenhousemuir, signals the start of the game. Immediately the Light Blues press forward. A centre from Bennett... and the Rangers have scored with a shot from Reid! One-nil to the home team! But the Hearts players protest and the referee consults with his linesman…who agrees with Mr Murray. The goal stands.

Galvanised, the Hearts attack. Wilson, on the run, gathers in the ball beautifully. He dashes deep into the Rangers half, and shoots on a tight angle. Lock blocks and recovers the ball, but Gracie follows up for the Hearts and bundles the ball and keeper over the line. Now the Rangers players protest. The referee waves their objections away. One-one here at Ibrox – both goals mired in controversy.

This is an excellent game. But it's the Hearts who look stronger. They've found their feet, despite this foul weather.

Wilson collects the ball on the left – he's having a most useful game. He beats Kelso and fires in a cross. Gracie just fails to reach the ball – but Wattie is there! Two-one to the Tynecastle men! Wattie stretched to the full and succeeded in scraping the ball past Lock in goal. He may have hurt himself in so doing.

The Rangers attack desperately – time is running out. But the Hearts defence stands up well. Scott has filled Mercer's position well today – a titanic performance!

The final whistle sounds. The Heart of Midlothian have beaten the Rangers two-one and their terrific winning run continues. With the Celtic dropping a point at Hibernian the question remains: Who can stop the men in maroon this season?

The Angel [*Reading from a newspaper*] 'How long is this craze of football to remain with us? How long are we to permit this miserable exhibition of spectacular blaggardism to sap the intellect of our young men? Let us legislate for conscription without delay and so put an end to this veritable curse. Letter to the Press.'

Briggs There would be no conscription until 1916. But more and more men volunteered... many never had the chance tae come back and see their team again. But we'll get to that...

Briggs starts leading the audience to the next scene.

The Angel Where are you off to? You coward! You should be ashamed of yourself, playing a daft game when good men are risking their lives for us... for YOU!

The Angel hands Briggs a white feather, a symbol of cowardice. She walks away.

Briggs [*To The Angel*] I'm no' a coward! I'll prove it! [*To the audience*] Come on, I'll take ye' back a bit further...

Briggs follows The Angel, who is playing her fiddle. He leads the audience around to the concourse of the Wheatfield Stand and down past the community pitches. Hearts players are being put through their paces by John McCartney. The Angel plays a burst of the Hearts song when they are seen. The journey continues to the Home dressing room.

Briggs Not many people get tae see in here. But I think you should. It's important... It's where our story really begins... I thought they'd be here by now though...

John McCartney enters the dressing room. We are back in August 1914, at the start of the season. His tone is curter than before.

McCartney Ah, Briggs. Good to see you've made it on time. We have introductions to make.

The sound of studs and banter can be heard in the corridor. A group of Hearts players enter the dressing room, in full strips: Patrick Crossan, Annan Ness, Harry Wattie, Duncan Currie and Ernie Ellis.

Jimmy Speedie, James Boyd, and Robert Mercer are played by The Angel.

McCartney Alfie Briggs, let me introduce Patrick Crossan.

Currie Paddy to the press.

Ellis Pat to his mates.

Ness Right-back.

Crossan The handsomest man in football.

Wattie The self-proclaimed handsomest man in football.

Currie Quickest man in Scotland over a hundred yards, they say.

Ness One o' the best passers in the game.

Wattie Aye, Pat can maybe pass the ball...but he couldnae pass a mirror if he tried!

McCartney This comedian is Harry Wattie.

Ellis Midfield general.

Currie When Bobby Walker retired, Gorgie was in woe!

Ness Then along came Harry.

Crossan In his debut against Rangers, he ran the show.

Ellis Scored two goals.

Currie Bobby Walker himself said, 'the gaffer's found a good 'un'.

Wattie I'm no Bobby Walker, but I'll take that!

McCartney This is James Speedie.

The Angel Jimmy!

McCartney James. We already have another Jimmy.

Currie Another impressive League debut.

Crossan Scored twice against Airdrieonians.

Ellis We won three-one!

Ness That was his only first team appearance last year though.

Currie Standing in for Willie Wilson.

Ellis Signed on as an amateur.

Wattie Aye, he didnae like the idea of turning professional!

The Angel Aye, but I had my reasons...I have my principles...

Currie Dinnae listen Jimmy, you stick in there.

McCartney Duncan Currie.

Ness Full-back.

Ellis Hairdresser by trade.

Crossan Handy boy to know...keeps us looking good, eh lads?

Wattie The gaffer actually tried to sign his older brother, Sam.

Ellis But he was nicked by Leicester.

Currie My dad was raging.

Ness So, Currie Senior promised the gaffer first refusal on his next son.

Currie I was the better prospect anyway!

The Angel Aye, Scotland will be knocking on your door soon!

McCartney Introducing Jimmy Boyd.

Ness His brother Archie is the keeper.

Ellis Young Boyd hasn't broken into the first team yet.

Crossan But he will. Eh son?

The Angel Aye!

Currie The gaffer said young Boyd put him in mind of Bobby Walker.

Wattie Another one? Christ!

Crossan High praise indeed.

Ness Jimmy'll get his chance. Trust me, I can see it!

McCartney This visionary is Annan Ness.

Crossan He hails all the way from deepest, darkest...

Wattie Fife!

Ness Kirkcaldy.

Ellis Exotic!

Currie Originally a miner.

Crossan Then a soldier.

Currie Then a Hearts man!

Wattie He's a better soldier than he is a footballer!

Ness Aye, aye...

Crossan The gaffer spied him playing for Bonnyrigg Rose.

Ellis He's certainly bloomed since then...

Beat

Wattie I'll do the jokes pal.

McCartney Ernie Ellis.

Currie An Englishman!

Wattie A Sassenach!

Crossan Born and bred in Norfolk.

Ness Aye...and I'm meant tae be the exotic one!

Currie He's well-travelled, right enough.

Wattie Norwich.

Crossan To Barnsley.

Ness To Edinburgh. And the Hearts.

Ellis Yep. I kept moving in the right direction.

Wattie Aye. North!

The Angel Solid as the old castle rock.

Crossan Here he is.

McCartney Robert Mercer.

The Angel Bob.

Ellis Big Bob.

Ness Captain.

Wattie One o' the best defenders in the game.

Currie Defenders are meant tae clear their lines.

Ness No Bob.

Currie He controls, dribbles, passes oot o' danger.

Ellis There's nobody quite like him.

Crossan Burnley, Aston Villa and Manchester United have all tried tae sign him.

The Angel Aye. And the gaffer said...

All 'Get tae fu...'

McCartney All right boys, gather round.

The players gather round McCartney as he silently gives a team talk, complete with big gestures to make this obvious. Briggs speaks directly to the audience.

Briggs Little did we know then where this team was going. We finished third in the League the previous season, with a club record fifty-four points. In early June, we defeated a Danish International XI two-one on an overseas tour. We were flying! Three weeks later, Gavrilo Princip assassinated Archduke Franz Ferdinand in Sarajevo. This started a chain of events that had a massive impact, no' just on Scottish football, but on the whole world.

Crossan On the twenty-eighth of July, Austria-Hungary declared war on Serbia.

Currie The next day, Russia, in support of Serbia, mobilised against Austria-Hungary.

Ellis Two days later, Germany, in support of Austria-Hungary, declared war on Russia.

Ness Germany went on to attack Luxembourg and declared war on France.

The Angel When Belgium refused to let Germany cross her borders to invade France, Germany declared war on them too.

Wattie In support of Belgium, Britain declared war on Germany on the fourth of August.

Briggs Eleven days later, champions Celtic came to Tynecastle Park on the opening day of the new season.

Behind Briggs, the team talk bursts into vocal life. Briggs joins the lads; he is part of the team.

McCartney Briggs, you protect the area if Mercer pushes forward. Now, my boys. Do not fear what lies ahead out there. Look out for your mates. You are a team.

A unit. You must protect each other. You must fight for each other. You know the plan. Follow that plan and you can win. You WILL win! Get stuck in lads! Let's show everyone what we are made of. Let's show them that our Hearts will beat everyone and everything in our path! [*The boys cheer*] I'll see you out there.

McCartney leaves the dressing room. The Angel, as Speedie, clears her throat to speak, but the boys are too busy with the banter.

The Angel Lads. LADS! [*The boys stop talking, surprised*] Can I have your attention?...

Beat. The boys laugh.

Wattie Oh, wheesht boys, Mr Speedie has an announcement tae make!

Ellis What is it James?

Crossan Are you gonnae sing us a wee song?

The Angel I'm thinking of volunteering.

The banter stops.

Currie For the war?

The Angel Of course the bloody war, what else?

Ness But you can't.

The Angel I can. And I will.

Ness No, I mean you can't. You're no' allowed to. You'll break your contract with the club.

Crossan He's an amateur, remember?

Beat

Ness You still can't. It's dangerous.

Briggs [*Almost to himself*] He's just a laddie.

The Angel I'm old enough. And I'm not scared.

Ellis No one said you were pal.

Currie Are ye' sure?

The Angel Aye. I have my principles.

Beat

The Angel Just thought you should know.

The Angel exits the dressing room, leaving the boys stunned.

Crossan I dinnae believe it.

Wattie He does have his principles, eh.

Currie I've been thinking about it too.

Wattie [*Trying to be funny*] Aye? Sure you're no' just saying that because wee Jimmy said it first?

Ellis Not now, Harry, eh.

Wattie Aye, alright.

Currie No, I mean it. I know we cannae because we're professionals, but that doesnae mean I havenae thought about it.

A pause hangs in the air.

Ness Anyone else?

Crossan I dunno, like.

Beat

Wattie I will if yous will.

There is a ripple of agreement.

Briggs Well, maybe someone should speak to the gaffer? Tell him how we feel?

Ellis Annan, you used to be a soldier.

Ness So?

Ellis Dunno... it'll maybe have more clout coming from you.

McCartney bursts through the door.

McCartney Am I interrupting? [*The lads stand, not knowing what to say*] It's almost time for kick off! We've got a team of champions to beat, Speedie can't do it by himself! Get out there!

The boys exit the dressing room. Ness hangs back. Briggs remains, watching on.

Ness Guv'nor, can I have a quick word?

McCartney No!

Ness It's Speedie. He's talking about volunteering for the war.

McCartney What? What do the rest of the lads think?

Ness We want to do our bit too, Boss. We're no' cowards.

McCartney I see. But you can't. It's a legal minefield.

Ness Is there really nothing we...

McCartney Annan. Our hands are tied.

Beat

Ness Boss...

McCartney What now?!

Ness Any chance o' me making the first team? You said I've been improving.

McCartney Your time will come. On you go.

Ness But Boss...

McCartney Get tae...

Ness Aye, aye...

Ness exits. McCartney stands, deep in thought. Briggs sits beside him.

Briggs As you've already heard, we beat reigning champions Celtic two-nil that day. And we continued tae win. We disposed of Hibs, we saw off Rangers... but the press certainly tried tae stop us.

McCartney [*Reading from a newspaper*] 'This is no time for football. The nation must occupy itself with more serious business. The young men who play football, and those who look on, have better work to do.

They are summoned to leave their sport and play their part in a greater game. That game is war. For life and death. *London Evening News*.'

Briggs We couldnae let them affect us. We had the Falkirk game to think about.

Briggs and McCartney act as if watching the game from the dugout.

Commentator *Welcome back to Tynecastle Park for this vital League clash between the home team Heart of Midlothian and Falkirk.*

Wilson, on the left, shoots – it deflects off the Falkirk defender Reilly – past the 'Bairns' keeper Stewart into the net! The opening goal for the Hearts! The crowd celebrate on the terraces!

Spurred on, the Hearts attack again. A snap shot – this time Stewart saves well! The Hearts' aggression is proving too much for Falkirk.

At the interval, the Hearts lead by that solitary goal. The Queen's Own Cameron Highlanders are here today, appealing for volunteers to help the war effort.

The second half is underway. Another fine tackle there for Scott! Once again he has deputised ably for Mercer, the injured captain, who's unlikely to be seen again in the field this season. Scott collects the ball and plays it forward. It rebounds off Orrock via Gracie to Wattie – who smashes the ball home! No chance for the 'Bairns' keeper this time! Hearts celebrate their second goal, richly deserved!

And that's the end of the match! Another win for the unbeaten Tynecastle men, a decided improvement on recent displays and that's nineteen wins from twenty-one games for the Heart of Midlothian. But for the Falkirk keeper, they might have scored more heavily.

Victory maintains their position at the top of the table. The Celtic, their nearest rivals, accounted for Third Lanark and remain four points in arrears.

Briggs Final score, Heart of Midlothian two, Falkirk nil.

The Angel enters.

The Angel 'While Hearts continue to play football, enabled thus to pursue their peaceful play by the sacrifice of the lives of thousands of their countrymen, they might adopt, temporarily, a *nom de plume*, say, "the White Feathers of Midlothian". Soldier's Daughter, *Edinburgh Evening News.*'

The Angel exits.

Briggs The White Feathers of Midlothian.

Sir George McCrae enters the dressing room. He is confident and forward, taking McCartney by surprise.

McCrae Ah, Mr McCartney, here you are. I was waiting for you in your office, but I became restless.

McCartney You were in my...

McCrae Office. Yes. I couldn't help but notice the framed quote above your desk. 'You must always cut your coat according to your cloth.'

McCartney Uh...yes...that was on the wall when I arrived here...

McCrae It's safe, isn't it? Cautious. Not an ambitious philosophy.

McCartney I thought so too.

McCrae But what really caught my eye, was the handwritten note attached to the frame. Your handiwork, I believe, Mr McCartney? 'Always give the public what the public wants!' Incredible! Indicative of your team's exploits on the field, dare I say.

McCartney Thank you, Mr...?

McCrae McCrae. [*Extending his hand*] George McCrae.

Beat

McCartney I wasn't expecting such esteemed company, Sir George...

McCrae Ach away! It is I who am honoured! I'm an old Hearts man, I get along when I can. And your boys are playing some of the best football I've ever seen. However, it is not the football that brings me here this day. You will be aware, no doubt, of our plight on the Western Front. And the shortage of manpower we have at our disposal.

McCartney The whole country is aware, Sir George.

McCrae Prospects are bleak, Mr McCartney. And as such, your club and its players have come under some scrutiny, dare I say.

McCartney Well, yes. That's the price they are paying for leading the League.

McCrae The newspapers are printing damning articles about them.

McCartney Not only that, they are receiving letters accusing them of cowardice. They are not cowards by a long chalk, Sir George.

McCrae That young lad, Speedie, volunteered did he not?

McCartney Aye. James. And Neil Moreland and George Sinclair were recalled to their regiments. We are all proud of them. The rest of the boys are keen to volunteer, but the club is bound contractually to the players. Forcing them to enlist would be illegal. And if they volunteer, the players would be in breach of their contracts. Our hands are tied.

McCrae And if those ties had been loosened?

McCartney I'm not sure I understand, Sir George.

McCrae I have been given permission by the War Office to raise a battalion, here in Edinburgh. I intend to raise over a thousand men in seven days.

McCartney Seven days? That's impossible.

McCrae Nothing is impossible, Mr McCartney.

McCartney What can we do?

McCrae Allow your boys to volunteer.

McCartney Apart from that.

McCrae Dare I say...

McCartney Like I said before, Sir George, there is nothing we can do; the contract situation makes it impossible...

McCrae Like I said before, Mr McCartney, nothing is impossible. At this time, their contract should be to their country, not their club. Your team, your boys, are the best in the land...

McCartney And we have a League to win.

McCrae We have a WAR to win.

Beat

McCartney has a flash of realisation.

McCartney And if my boys volunteer, the fans will follow. That's one hell of a recruiting tool.

McCrae You catch on fast Mr McCartney. 'Always give the public what the public wants!'

Beat

McCrae I am proud of what you and your boys have achieved this season. And as such, I have assurances from the War Office that if any of these men volunteer for my battalion, they will serve together for the duration of the conflict. They will get to fight alongside their pals. You have my word.

McCartney pauses. The gravity of the situation is sinking in.

McCartney I assume the directors have made their feelings known.

McCrae They have.

McCartney Then this is not a matter for me.

McCrae No. It is a matter for King and Country.

McCartney I will speak to the players, inform them of their options. Then you can speak to them about your battalion.

McCrae Thank you, Mr McCartney. You're a good man.

McCrae leaves. McCartney stands, deep in thought once more. The sound of studs can be heard once more as the boys enter the dressing room.

McCartney Take a seat, boys. There was a board meeting last night. It was decided, unanimously, that no obstacle be placed in the way of any player desiring to volunteer.

Currie Aye?

Wattie Really?

McCartney Really.

Ness What about our contracts?

McCartney You will continue to be paid in full if you play, and be paid half wages if you are unable to play due to military commitments.

Crossan And what if we end up going away?

McCartney If you return fit and well from the war, you will be re-engaged on your old terms. Can I ask those who were willing to volunteer to be upstanding.

Beat

The boys look to each other and all stand.

McCartney [*Half smiling, even though it is hard for him*] Thought as much.

The boys file out of the dressing room. McCartney follows and The Angel plays her fiddle. Briggs leads the audience up the tunnel to the Wheatfield Stand. This is now in the Usher Hall. McCrae addresses the audience directly. While he does so, the players gather behind him.

McCrae This is not a night for titles. I stand before you humbly as a fellow Scot. Nothing more and nothing less. You know I don't speak easily of crisis, but that is what confronts us. I have received permission from the War Office to raise a new battalion for active service. It is my intention that this unit will reflect accurately all the many classes of this famous capital, and that it will be characterised by such a spirit of excellence that the rest of Lord Kitchener's army will be judged by our standard. Furthermore, with the agreement of the authorities, I have undertaken to lead the battalion in the field. I would not - I could not - ask you to serve unless I share the danger at your side. In a moment I will walk down to Castle Street and set my name to the list of volunteers. Who will join me?

The players step forward, falling in line with McCrae, who then goes down the line and shakes each of their hands, thanking them. As he does, The Angel sings the following to the tune of 'Scots Wha Hae' and accompanies on her fiddle.

Song Who would bear a sword unsheathed
While the guilty Kaiser breathed?
Rise wi' vengeance steeled and teethed,
Strike wi' George McCrae.
Who for Britain's realm would stand,
Fechtin' bravely man tae man?
Freeman rise and in the van
Gang wi' George McCrae.

As the song ends, McCrae salutes and he and the boys march out, except Briggs.

Briggs There was a crowd o' more than 4,000 in the Usher Hall that night. Almost all of the men followed Sir George down Lothian Road to the recruiting office on Castle Street. Myself and the boys were joined by players from other teams too. Lads from Hibs, Dunfermline, Raith Rovers, Falkirk, East Fife and many more joined the cause. In turn, the supporters of these clubs also volunteered, inspired by their sporting heroes. It didnae take long for the battalion to reach its target. Our military training began straight away.

The players enter, running into formation, as if on a training drill. The next movement section emulates the training as well as the football matches.

Currie Up at 6am, run a hundred yards in the cold dark frosty mornings with towel around neck to a tap around which about thirty men are struggling to wash.

Ellis Dash back; make up blankets and mattress, then parade.

Wattie Breakfast 9am - kipper and two ounces white bread plus coffee.

Crossan Then there are the nocturnal expeditions!

Ness By the left, quick march!

Briggs It seems that battalions on the front often have to travel considerable distances under cover of darkness.

Ness We are therefore putting in some practice.

Currie It is a tiring business, but we have learned the art of sleeping on the march.

Wattie You simply shut your eyes and hope that the fellow in front has his wits about him.

Ellis After a pleasant hour or so, you awake to find yourself in some forlorn village chosen for its treacherous approaches.

Ness I am sure that the natives in these places consider us mad.

Ellis They may be right, but we are also very fit and getting fitter by the day.

Briggs Last night, well on after ten, we took a breather outside Carlops.

Crossan It was very dark and there was a sharp frost, but we had brought the lamps so we could warm our hands and see at the same time.

Currie Carlops is a five-hour march from Edinburgh. We returned to our digs well on after 3am.

Ness Later that morning, after little sleep, we got the train to Glasgow to face Celtic.

The boys watch the empty pitch, reacting to the game.

Commentator *The keenly anticipated return League contest between the Heart of Midlothian and the Celtic took place on Saturday at Glasgow, and the result was a draw. Consequently, the clubs remain as they were in the competition for the Championship. Both have eleven matches still to play, and the Hearts are four points to the good, but they have a more difficult road to traverse than their rivals before the flag is safely won. The Hearts had rather less of the game than the Celts, and did well to draw. The Celtic were strong in defence, but very weak* *near their opponents' goal. For the Hearts the defence was also the better part of the team, the half-backs in particular playing grandly. The forwards were poor, but when they got to goal they were a more dangerous lot than the Celtic five.*

When the circumstances of the time are taken into consideration it was remarkable that close to 52,000 people should have been present at the match, and from start to finish their interest was sustained to the highest pitch.

Briggs Final score...Celtic one, Heart of Midlothian one.

Wattie We are turning out to play in new boots.

Briggs Boots that are one size bigger than normal to accommodate the bloody blisters we have on our feet!

Ness Regardless, our military training doesn't desist.

Currie Our trainer, Jimmy Duckworth, started coming with us on our marches.

Ellis Duckie said he wanted to be there to treat any injuries we get.

Wattie He's sixty-three!

Crossan Aye, and the cold didnae agree with him. His lungs are playing up and he's in bed.

Currie We were marched out to Balerno in the freezing cold, returning at 10pm, only to be up at six for more drills.

Ellis The boys are dropping like flies with the flu.

Wattie We got our second round of inoculations. Typhoid this time.

Crossan Two days later, the Rangers came to Tynecastle.

Currie The injections caused a bout of vomiting in the dressing room at half-time.

Crossan, Wattie, Currie and Briggs turn round to be sick.

Ness Crossan, Wattie, Currie and Briggs only came back out for the second half because there was no one else to take their places!

The players gradually leave during the following commentary, leaving Briggs alone.

Commentator *24,000 spectators have convened at Tynecastle today where the League leaders welcome the Rangers.*

Reid for the Rangers looks lively, he accepts a pass, he scores! The visiting fans cheer ecstatically! A slackness is evident in the Hearts defence today.

Another blunder from Currie – and Cairns is in. Goal! Two-nil for the Rangers!

The Hearts respond, attacking with pace. Good work from Crossan. The Rangers defence are hard-pressed. Craig tackles again in great style. He plays it to Reid...who scores again! Three-nil! Disaster for the Hearts men.

And Reid has the ball...He's scored another! That's his hat-trick. He's made the points absolutely safe for his team. Four-nil to the Rangers. Oh the Hearts must be broken. But here they gallantly attack again, and a penalty is awarded. Gracie steps up...

and scores! A consolation goal at least.

Briggs plays the ball to Low – an express drive from the Hearts forward, what a goal! The result looks more respectable now. Straight from the restart, Hearts retain possession. Wilson traps the ball expertly, and hits a long swerving shot – it's in! The goalkeeper was helpless! three goals in... I make it eight minutes. An incredible come-back! Four-three to the Rangers. They look rattled and the Hearts desperately attack once more. The final minute of the match. Willie Wilson has the ball – he hits a fierce drive – Lock is beaten all ends up – but it hits the post! – the roars of 'goal' are stifled as the ball rebounds away to safety for the Rangers. And the referee whistles to signal the end of the match. A stirring finish to a notable game.

Today is a significant day in the Scottish Football League, for the Heart of Midlothian have suffered their first defeat at Tynecastle this season. With the Celtic beating Dumbarton, the Parkhead team are now only two points behind their Edinburgh rivals.

Briggs Final score, Heart of Midlothian three, Rangers four.

The Angel 'No one wants to belittle the performance of the Rangers at Tynecastle, but it is undoubted fact that military training is having a certain effect on the Heart of Midlothian players.'

Briggs Aye... you're no' kidding!

The Angel 'While the men have lost none of their footballing ability, and have probably gained in stamina, they have certainly lost in speed. Military training, such as they are going for, certainly tends to bind and harden the muscles, and in the early stages of a game the men are probably a yard or two slower than what they were in normal times. *Evening Times.*'

Briggs The following week, we crossed the city tae face Hibs. Despite beating them six-nil earlier in the season, we were held to a two-all draw. We took the lead, but we were exhausted and couldnae hold on. Meanwhile, Celtic were beating Partick Thistle two-nil. They were now only one point behind us.

The audience is led from the Wheatfield Stand seats to the concourse behind. McCartney and the boys, apart from Ness, are already there. They are visibly exhausted and upset. Army uniforms are in piles around the space. McCartney reads from a newspaper.

McCartney 'Only the team's great fighting spirit saw them through the programme after Christmas. They played at times so tired and sore that they could hardly stand; yet they took Celtic to the last day of the season and left Rangers floundering eleven points behind. They gave their best throughout and that is all that anyone could ask.'

The newspaper is passed between the players as they read a section. They also begin to change into their army uniforms.

Briggs 'Saturday saw an end to the struggle between the Heart of Midlothian and the Celtic for the Scottish League Championship. The former lost at Paisley, and the Celtic won at Cathkin, and stand three points ahead with a match still to play. The Hearts have completed their programme...'

Crossan 'The Parkhead team are to be congratulated on retaining possession of the flag, but much sympathy will go out to the Hearts, who put up a great fight, and at one time seemed almost certain champions.'

Wattie 'What effect military training may have on the form of footballers is a matter for argument, but the fact remains that it was only after the majority of the Tynecastle players had enlisted that a deterioration of play set in.'

Ellis 'Fully 7,000 spectators saw the Heart of Midlothian suffer defeat at Paisley in their last League engagement of the season. They attacked almost constantly, and Graham, Briggs, Bryden and Wattie all had good tries at goal. But the St Mirren defence was very sound.'

Currie 'Both goalkeepers were tested before Sowerby dropped in a great centre, which Clark, rushing in, swept into the net. The home team played with great confidence after this score...Though the Hearts rallied for a final effort, in the end St. Mirren had won on their merits.'

Ness enters in full uniform, carrying Glengarries for the rest of the boys.

The Angel 'Hearts have laboured these past weeks under a dreadful handicap, the like of which our friends in the West cannot imagine. There is only one football champion in Scotland, and its colours are maroon and khaki.'

The Angel plays a solitary note on her fiddle. Ness, inspired by the sound, begins to sing.

Ness Come pack up your footballs and scarves of maroon,
Leave all your sweethearts in Auld Reekie toon,
Fall in wi' the lads for we're off and away,
To take on the Hun with Old Geordie McCrae.

The rest of the boys gradually join in, until everyone is singing with meaning. During the song, the lads place their football boots and Hearts jerseys in a line and form a tableau, resembling the famous 1914 team photograph.

All Come pack up your footballs and scarves of maroon,
Leave all your sweethearts in Auld Reekie toon,
Fall in wi' the lads for we're off and away,
To take on the Hun with Old Geordie McCrae.

Kaiser Bill he came marching o'er Belgium and France,
To challenge the Empire with warlike advance.
So the bravest of Hearts volunteered for the fray
And threw in their lot with old Geordie McCrae!

Come pack up your footballs and scarves of maroon,
Leave all your sweethearts in Auld Reekie toon,
Fall in wi' the lads for they're off and away,
To take on the Hun with Old Geordie McCrae.

Oh, it's sad to be leaving but happy to go,
Now it's up wi' the Colonel and down wi' the foe.
And when victory's ours we'll be able to say,
That we fought by the side of old Geordie McCrae.

Come pack up your footballs and scarves of maroon,
Leave all your sweethearts in Auld Reekie toon,
Fall in wi' the lads for they're off and away,
To take on the Hun with Old Geordie McCrae.

The boys bid farewell to McCartney, handing their jerseys to him. Briggs is the last to do so. The lads file off down the concourse to the stairs and the trench.

Briggs [*To the audience*] Right folks! We're off tae France! Follow me!

McCartney is left alone. The Angel leads the audience down the concourse to the Western Front.

ACT TWO

Away, 27 January 1916

A trench sits in between the Wheatfield and Roseburn Stands.

The lads are settled in the trench. They tie up their puttees while the audience gets settled. They are still buoyant and conversational. The Angel watches on.

Briggs We left the football fields o' Tynecastle, Easter Road and Starks Park for the battlefields o' France.

Crossan Well, most of us.

Ellis James Speedie was already away.

Currie He'd left for Loos in July with the 7th Cameron Highlanders.

Ness We, however, were headed for the front line town of Armentières.

Wattie [*Singing*] Mademoiselle from Armentières, parlez-vous?

All [*Singing*] Mademoiselle from Armentières,
parlez-vous?
Mademoiselle from Armentières,
She hasn't been kissed for forty years,
Hinky dinky parlez-vous!

Mademoiselle from Armentières, parlez-vous?
Mademoiselle from Armentières, parlez-vous?
She'll do it for wine, she'll do it for rum,
And sometimes for chocolate and chewing gum,
Hinky dinky parlez-vous!

Mademoiselle from Armentières, parlez-vous?
Mademoiselle from Armentières, parlez-vous?
She was true to me, she was true to you,
She was true to the whole damn army too!
Hinky dinky parlez-vous!

Wattie We marched in on the twenty-seventh of January 1916.

Briggs It was cold.

Crossan Bloody cold!

Ellis And it was the Kaiser's birthday!

The Angel plays a quick burst of 'Happy Birthday'. Sarcastic cheers from the boys.

Ness Fritz had a celebration planned.

Crossan Champagne?

Currie Cake?

Wattie Dancing girls?

Briggs Fireworks, mair like.

An explosion. The sound of shelling starts.

Crossan They lit up the sky with the heaviest shelling ever seen in the area.

Ellis Happy bloody birthday, Bill!

Wattie Arse!

Currie The noise was deafening.

Ness Then all of a sudden, it stopped.

Silence

Currie And the machine guns started.

The rattle of machine gun fire starts.

Briggs At first, every ping of a bullet makes you duck your heid.

Crossan But you soon get used tae it.

The machine guns stop.

Ellis After it died down, we were hit with this peculiar, heavy, drowsy feeling.

Wattie Like getting an uppercut from the Sandman.

Ness It's normal after close range artillery fire.

Currie Who'd have known gunfire could be a lullaby?

The lads begin to relax and the shelling starts again. They moan and groan. Suddenly, a much louder, closer explosion rocks the trench. Off, a voice can be heard calling for help. Ness runs off.

Ness [*Off*] Jesus Christ!

Briggs What?

Ness [*Off*] All the flying earth fae that shell has spoiled our butter!

Wattie Aye, well it's lucky it didnae spoil us.

Ness enters holding up Leonard, who is dazed from the explosion.

Ness It nearly spoiled him. I found him half buried in the mud.

Crossan Ah, you must be Jack Johnson.

Wattie Did you fly in on the Ypres Express?

Leonard Whit?

Ness Doesnae matter son. Are ye' alright?

Leonard I think so.

Ness I'm Sergeant Major Annan Ness. Welcome to the Somme. What's your name?

Leonard Leonard. Private John Leonard, sir.

Leonard stands up and salutes and is hauled back down by the boys.

Ness Enough of the 'sir' nonsense, we're all the same doon here. Meet the rest of the boys. This is Pat Crossan.

Crossan The handsomest soldier in the battalion.

Wattie The self-proclaimed handsomest soldier in the battalion!

Ness This comedian is Harry Wattie. Resident storyteller Alfie Briggs. Duncan Currie, the demon barber of Armentières.

Wattie And the Sassenach in the corner is Ernie Ellis.

Ellis doesn't respond; he seems distant.

Leonard I know you lot! You play for Hearts!

Wattie Oh...we're famous! Tell me, Johnny boy, do you go to the games?

Leonard Well...actually, I follow Hibs.

The lads stop what they are doing and stare at Leonard.

Currie Oh dear.

Wattie That just won't do, John.

A couple of the lads cock their rifles. The silence hangs long enough for him to feel nervous before the lads start laughing.

Briggs We're only pulling your leg, Johnny boy! We're all on the same team here.

Ness Where are you from?

Leonard Kirk Street. Foot of the Walk. I'm a wages clerk. Well, I was. [*To Ness*] What do you do back home?

Again, the lads stop what they are doing, but there is a silent air of amusement this time.

Ness I play for Hearts as well.

Leonard Oh. It's just that I dinnae recognise you.

The lads try, without much luck, to supress their laughter.

Currie He plays in the reserves.

Crossan But he's still a cracking player.

Wattie A better soldier than a footballer though, eh 'Sir'?

Ness Aye, lucky for you...'Private'.

Briggs Oi, I thought we were all the same in here!

The shelling comes to an end, only to be replaced once again by machine gun fire. Leonard drops to the floor. Nobody else flinches.

Wattie Easy, Johnny boy, they're just saying 'guten morgen'.

Ness It's ok, pal.

Leonard Still no' used tae it.

Briggs Puts me in mind of the sound of rivets. It's what I did before I turned professional. I always liked the sound before. Now I hate it.

Leonard Right! [*To Currie, who is cutting Crossan's hair*] What did you do before?

Currie [*Without looking up*] I was a surgeon.

Leonard Really? [*He twigs*] Oh aye, very good!

Crossan It's the rats I hate.

Leonard Rats?

Crossan Aye. Big bastards.

Currie Mair like cats than rats.

Crossan Crawl all over you when you're trying tae sleep.

Wattie Good thing you cannae get any sleep then, eh!

Currie I hate the cold. Rubbing anti-frostbite on your feet.

Briggs The rain.

Currie The mud.

Wattie Drying socks!

All Oh aye!

Wattie Seems we do more drying that fighting, eh! [*He hits Ellis over the head with a soaking wet sock and Ellis jumps up and pushes him*]

Ellis Does everything have to be a bloody joke to you? Is drying bloody socks the worst of your worries? [*Wattie puts his hand on Ellis's shoulder, which is duly shrugged off*] Get your hands off me!

Ness steps in between the men. Ellis storms out. Ness follows him.

Briggs [*To Leonard*] His wife just had a daughter.

Currie He was denied compassionate leave.

Briggs Can't be spared.

Leonard That's awful.

Crossan Add it tae the list.

There is a silence in the trench, despite the noise of distant shelling.

Currie I wish they'd let up, just for a while. Gies a wee break.

Crossan We should arrange another one of those truces, like they did last Christmas. Instead of fighting, we should take the Fritzes on at football. Winner takes all.

Currie Aye, we'd win this war in ninety minutes!

Leonard That sounds better than fighting.

Briggs I'd keep your voices down. You'll get hauled up in front o' the beaks.

Leonard Dinnae be daft!

Briggs I'm telling ye. After the big Christmas truce, the powers that be decided fraternisation with the enemy was not patriotic. Some commander in the Scots Guards was court-martialled for arranging a ceasefire while both sides buried their dead at Easter time. Got away with it, mind you.

Leonard Aye? How?

Briggs His wife's uncle is the Prime Minister. It's who you ken, eh.

Crossan They pin medals on you for killing Germans and court-martial you for being human. Doesnae make sense to me...

Ellis and Ness enter, the former looking sheepish.

Ellis Sorry lads. I shouldn't have done that. I was out of order. I've embarrassed myself.

The lads all accept his apology. Ellis goes to Wattie and holds out his hand.

Ellis I'm sorry Harry. Mates?

Wattie hugs him.

Wattie Dinnae be daft pal, it's forgotten. Save it for the Boche though, eh?

Suddenly, the machine gun fire ceases, to be replaced by the sound of Schubert, drifting over from the German trenches.

Wattie Oh Christ.

Currie No' again.

Leonard What's that?

Ness Schubert.

Briggs The Fritzes play him on their gramophones.

Crossan A lot.

Ness Symphony Number Eight.

Currie His unfinished symphony.

Wattie Christ, it's finished me off. [*Shouting*] Start the shelling again!

Ness [*To Wattie*] Heathen!

Leonard It's no' that bad.

Wattie It is when you've heard it a hundred times.

Ness Right lads, as much as I love a musical debate, while the Boche are on a tea break, we should see to the section o' trench that was hit by that Jack Johnson.

The boys protest, except Leonard who has a flash of realisation about Jack Johnson.

Shovels! I'll follow you the now, I'm going to get that letter to the Guv'nor finished.

Crossan Mind my melodeon!

Ness Aye, aye...

The lads file out past Ness. Ellis and Leonard bring up the rear.

Leonard What's your daughter's name?

Ellis Catherine. But we call her Kitty.

Leonard Kitty. That's a bonny name. Dinnae worry. You'll get to see her soon enough.

They exit, leaving Ness alone. He pulls some paper and a pencil from his pocket and begins to write.

Ness 'We came to the conclusion that the articles mentioned here are the most desired: a melodeon for Crossan...'

Crossan [*Off*] Cheers!

Ness 'A few mouth organs (to keep Fritz happy); socks (always); no underwear (please); chocolate, sweets, dried fruit; toilet soap; candles, matches, cigarettes, tobacco; old magazines; writing paper and envelopes. As the authorities are desirous that the men smoke pipes, could you send us some. The list need not be strictly adhered to. Anything will be appreciated. Annan Ness.'

Ness exits. The Angel plays a tune to show the passing of time. The lads enter. They are visibly more exhausted than before. Leonard in particular is in a bad way.

Ellis If I never see another bloody shovel as long as I live, it'll be too bloody soon.

Crossan Ken! All we seem tae dae is dig. That's been a fortnight o' digging!

Briggs Digging holes in bits o' France...

Currie To fill other holes in other bits o' France.

Wattie Aye? Most o' it's in my bloody boots.

There is a loud and sudden barrage of shelling. Leonard is more visibly shaken by this than the rest.

Briggs [*To the audience*] Twenty-fourth of June 1916. Just outside Contalmaison.

Ellis If the bloody Boche would stop shelling our handiwork, we wouldn't have to dig so much.

Currie It's no' fair, eh.

Wattie Ken. [*To Ness*] As the ranking soldier here, gonnae tell them to stop?

Ness Aye, I'll pop over no-man's-land the now.

Briggs Why do we keep firing on them?

Wattie Eh...we're at war with them! What the hell do you expect us tae dae? Blow kisses?

Briggs I ken that...I just mean, they have the high ground. We wind them up by firing at them, so they fire back. But we always end up worse off.

Currie Aye, and we cannae repair the damage properly without getting sniped at. Our trenches are a shambles.

Crossan We need a level playing field.

Ellis Like we had back at home, eh?

Leonard, who has sat separately from the rest, begins to sob, although he's trying not to show it. However, Ellis notices and goes to him.

Ellis Johnny boy?

Leonard I want tae go home, Ernie. I cannae take the noise anymore. I want tae go back to Kirk Street. I want my mum.

Ellis sits beside him, puts his arm around him.

Ellis I know pal. But we have a job to do. And the sooner we get the chance to do it, the sooner we get home.

Leonard I just want tae run.

Ellis That won't do you any good pal. Listen, I'm scared too. Really scared. But we'll be ok if we look out for each other. And, I think Kitty would like to meet her uncle Johnny when we get back. Together.

Leonard nods. During this exchange, The Angel hands two letters to Ness, who gestures to Briggs and Wattie to go offstage.

Ness Lads...Gather round. It's from the Gaffer.

'I hope this will suffice. Should you require anything else, please do not hesitate to ask. John McCartney.'

During the list, Briggs and Wattie return with some of the items which get handed out. Crossan gets his melodeon; a football, a few packs of cigarettes and harmonicas are passed out.

Ness We have: '240 pairs of socks; 141lb black tobacco; 12 dozen pipes; 5,000 cigarettes; 200 boxes of matches; 25 harmonicas; 2 fiddles; 100 boxes of Edinburgh Rock; 400 bars of Fry's milk chocolate;

300 candles; 20 cases of toilet soap; 12 dozen writing pads; 3,000 envelopes; 14 pairs of football boots; 3 balls; 2 pumps; 1 melodeon; [*The boys cheer*] assorted magazines and books. Also, a tin of Jean McCartney's special tablet for whoever needs it most'.

Wattie Johnny boy.

Wattie hands the tablet to Leonard, who is moved by the gesture.

Leonard Thanks lads.

A hipflask of King George IV whisky appears.

Wattie KG4 anyone?

Leonard What's that?

Ness It's King George IV whisky. It's distilled opposite Tynecastle.

Currie A wee taste o' home!

Crossan [*Pointing to his melodeon*] Lads! Guess what? Made in Germany!

The lads laugh. Then, the shelling abruptly stops, as if by design.

Wattie Gies a tune, handsome!

Crossan I dinnae ken how tae say this... but I cannae play one o' these things!

Wattie What dae ye' mean?

Crossan I just wanted one. I thought I could learn...

The boys all start laughing, poking fun at Crossan.

Wattie Alright, how about this one?

[*Singing*] Hey, Billy boy, are ye waukin yet?
Ye'll think the war's been won, I bet.

All [*Singing*] But your soldier men will be beat, ye ken,
When they meet wi' McCrae's in the morning!

Crossan starts playing the melodeon badly and is joined by a couple of the lads on harmonicas. Everyone joins in with gusto. During the frivolities, Ness reads the other letter.

Hey, Billy boy, are ye waukin yet?
Ye'll think the war's been won, I bet.
But your soldier men will be beat, ye ken,
When they meet wi' McCrae's in the morning!

Ness Boys... BOYS!

Everyone and everything stops.

Ness James Speedie's dead. He died at Loos.

There is a long pause. Leonard holds the hipflask of KG4, which he raises in toast.

Leonard Tae James.

He drinks and passes it to Ness, as The Angel plays a lament on her fiddle.

Ness Tae Jimmy.

Ness pulls a makeshift wooden cross from the trench and places a Hearts jersey over it. The lads watch on, numb. The hipflask does the rounds and each lad takes a drink. Suddenly, the shelling starts again, interrupting the solemnity. Wattie has had enough.

Wattie For Christ's sake, gies peace for one minute!

He stands up and tries to climb out of the trench. The boys have to physically restrain him.

Ellis Harry...

Wattie No! I've had it! I'm sick. I'm sick o' the rats. O' the rain and the mud. I'm sick of Schubert! I'm sick o' the shells and the guns and the shovels. I'm sick o' seeing men buried. I'm sick o' the noise! We cannae even have a bit of quiet to pay our bloody respects!

McCrae enters. He has the air of a man, miles away, strolling around his garden.

McCrae I'm sick of it too, Private. I too want it to be over. I too want to go home. And we will. Zero day has been agreed.

Leonard Zero day, Sir?

McCrae When we attack. When we go over the top. The date has been set for the twenty-ninth of June.

Briggs Five days.

McCrae Five days. There will be a continued and sustained artillery bombardment, for the next five days, to destroy the German trenches and machine guns along with the network of barbed wire protecting them. This bombardment will begin imminently.

Crossan What's five more days of noise eh?

McCrae Once the wire and the guns are taken care of, we advance forward and take the trenches. We go over the top at zero-seven-thirty hours. We will capture

German defences up to and including the first reserve line by zero-eight-eighteen .

Wattie [*Sarcastically*] Specific.

McCrae Then we will assault and take the intermediate position in front of the fortified village of Contalmaison by zero-eight-fifty-eight and carry on the attack to the east of the town. With any luck, we will be brewing up by the back of ten.

Ness Sir...what if the wire and the machine guns are not destroyed by zero-seven-thirty hours?

McCrae I really hope they are, Sergeant Major - we go over at zero-seven-thirty hours regardless. I suggest you look at page twelve of your Pay Books. There you will find a 'Short Form of Will'. Copy it out. Just in case.

Beat

McCrae Private Leonard, report to your patrol.

Leonard Yes, sir.

The boys say goodbye to Leonard as he leaves the trench. McCrae notices the hipflask in Wattie's hand.

McCrae Private Wattie...what's this?

Wattie stands up and holds the flask out to McCrae. He is waiting to be disciplined. McCrae swigs from the flask and hands it back.

McCrae Good luck, boys.

McCrae exits and the boys find a spot in the trench and take out their pay books. The noise of shelling continues, just as

McCrae said. The Angel plays to ease the nerves.

Wattie Twenty-seventh of June 1916. In the event of my death, I give the whole of my property and effects to my mother, Mrs Wattie, 8 Livingstone Place, Edinburgh. Signed Henry Benzie Wattie. Private, number 19112, 16th Royal Scots.

Briggs The boys are not in the best of spirits. There is terrible artillery work going on and Fritz must be in a dreadful plight. I do not think it will be long ere we get home for good.

Ness Twenty-eighth of June. Arial reconnaissance has shown that our insistent shelling is not making adequate progress. Then the rain came down once more. It is so relentless that the attack has been postponed for forty-eight hours. The bombardment has been also been extended. Two extra days of noise.

Currie Twenty-ninth of June 1916. Father. The rest of the lads are busy making their wills. I, however, will not. It is not necessary or needed. I will be home soon enough. Your loving son, Duncan.

Crossan We can't sleep and the ground will not keep still. Don't be alarmed if you don't get a letter from me. I will try and manage a field postcard now and then.

Ellis Thirtieth of June 1916. To my dear daughter Kitty, I leave my half-loop lady's ring and my gold chain. I would also like it if her mother would give her the pick of the rings I gave her before we married. To my darling wife, I leave my gold wedding ring. [*Pause*] If it is recovered from my body. Signed Ernest Ellis. Private, number 19009, 16th Royal Scots.

Leonard enters, looking visibly shaken like before.

Wattie Where have ye' been, Johnny boy?

Ellis We were worried about you.

Leonard Last night, I was part of a patrol that crawled into no-man's-land to check the German wire. We were discovered just after midnight.

Crossan What happened?

Currie Are ye' hurt?

Leonard I'm fine. But we lost four men. Another two were wounded.

Ness What's the damage?

Leonard The wire's pretty much intact. The machine guns tae.

Beat

I'd better report back...and lads, thanks for...you know...looking after me. I'll see yous after, eh?

Leonard exits.

Wattie A week of constant shelling, and it's no' made a difference.

The noise of shelling stops. It is time.

Ness Right lads. It's time for kick off. Check your gear.

There is a moment of silence, while each lad prepares in his own way; perhaps a check of rifles, or a whisper of prayer. Ness takes the football from the care package box and holds it for a moment. He quietly starts to sing, just as he did back at Tynecastle Park. The lads gradually join in.

Ness Come pack up your footballs and scarves of maroon,
Leave all your sweethearts in Auld Reekie toon,

All Fall in wi' the lads for we're off and away,
To take on the Hun with Old Geordie McCrae.

Oh, it's sad to be leaving but happy to go,
Now it's up wi' the Colonel and down wi' the foe.
And when victory's ours we'll be able to say,
That we fought by the side of old Geordie McCrae.

Come pack up your footballs and scarves of maroon,
Leave all your sweethearts in Auld Reekie toon,
Fall in wi' the lads for we're off and away...

They are interrupted by the shrill sound of a whistle.

The soldiers climb out of the trench and disappear out of sight. The noise of shelling and gunfire begins again, increasing to an overwhelming crescendo. Then it ceases.

The Angel leads the audience out of the trench and through the gates into the Memorial Garden.

The boys march in and place a poppy next to the memorial plaque of their character. They line up around the centrepiece of the garden.

Briggs The first of July 1916 remains the blackest day in British military history. The British suffered almost 60,000 casualties. Nearly 20,000 men died that day, Harry Wattie, Duncan Currie and Ernie Ellis among them. Their bodies were never found.

Briggs, Ness and Crossan turn to salute Wattie, Ellis and Currie, who march through the memorial garden doors.

Briggs Of the 814 men from McCrae's Battalion who had advanced, only 178 returned.

Crossan It was pure hell crossing that ground. The bullets were like hailstones. It was awful seeing all your chums go under and not being able to do anything for them.

Briggs Two weeks after the first day of the Somme, from his trench in France, Annan Ness wrote to his former manager John McCartney...

Ness *'We had a match the other evening, but oh Mr McCartney, we did miss the boys. Talk about football. It made the tears come to our eyes. But have a good heart, Guv'nor, we shall soon be in Berlin. My best regards to the directors and yourself.'*

Crossan When the war was over, one hundred surviving members of McCrae's Own were given complimentary season tickets. John McCartney wrote a tribute to his boys...

Briggs *'Voluntarily these men went forth to fight for King and Country. The gloomiest hour in the nation's history found them ready. As pioneers in the formation of a brilliant regiment, sportsmen the world over will remember them. Duty well and truly done, they are welcomed back to Tynecastle.'*

Ness In 1933, John McCartney passed away, as the world powers were gathering to march to war once more.

Crossan On the eleventh of November 1928, from the fireside of his home, Sir George McCrae wrote: *'In the flames I see the faces of my boys. So young and full of promise. The sorrow and the pride are overwhelming. Sorrow at the loss and pride in the manner of their dying.'*

Ness *'They never flinched. Faced by a veritable storm of shot and shell, they marched towards the guns beside their friends.'*

Briggs *'In remembering them, we must acknowledge our debt and find some way to justify our own lives so that when we meet our comrades in that better place, we are able to say with a brave heart that we did not let them down.'*

Ness Five weeks later, Sir George passed away. 150,000 people attended his funeral, still the largest event of its kind in Scotland's history.

Crossan Annan Ness survived the war. He cancelled his contract with Hearts on his return to pursue a career as a dentist, later becoming a dental surgeon. He died of cancer in an Edinburgh nursing home in 1942.

Ness leaves through the door to the stadium.

Briggs Paddy Crossan also came home from the trenches. He remained a first team regular at Tynecastle until 1925. Then he opened his pub, the famous 'Paddy's Bar'. He was the handsomest publican on Rose Street. He used to love a good blether at the bar and would stand his various friends several drinks; a better footballer than a publican. He died of pulmonary tuberculosis in 1933.

Crossan leaves.

Briggs And me? Well, I held on until 1950. I was forced tae retire from playing after what happened to me at the Somme. As well as the bullets in my back, one broke my right leg, another my left foot, another passed through my right arm, another shattered my knee. The last one glanced my forehead, knocking me unconscious. I lay half dead for two days. German soldiers crawled over me, thinking I was already gone. But I refused tae die. And home I came. And as long as I have a voice, I will tell this story. The story of the bravest team and the finest group of lads I have ever known. This is our story.

The Angel plays 'The Last Post' on the fiddle. Briggs takes off his Glengarry and places it on the centrepiece. He stands in tribute until The Angel finishes playing. After a moment, Briggs leaves.

The End.

TIPPERMUIR BOOKS

Tippermuir Books Ltd is an independent publishing company based in Perth, Scotland.

Publishing History

Spanish Thermopylae (2009)

Battleground Perthshire (2009)

Perth: Street by Street (2012)

Born in Perthshire (2012)

In Spain with Orwell (2013)

Trust (2014)

Perth: As Others Saw Us (2014)

Love All (2015)

A Chocolate Soldier (2016)

The Early Photographers of Perthshire (2016)

Taking Detective Novels Seriously: The Collected Crime Reviews of Dorothy L Sayers (2017)

Walking with Ghosts (2017)

No Fair City: Dark Tales from Perth's Past (2017)

The Tale o the Wee Mowdie that wantit tae ken wha keeched on his heid (2017)
Shortlisted for Scots Children's Book of the Year 2019

Hunters: Wee Stories from the Crescent: A Reminiscence of Perth's Hunter Crescent (2017)

A Little Book of Carol's (2018)

Flipstones (2018)

Perth: Scott's Fair City: The Fair Maid of Perth & Sir Walter Scott – A Celebration & Guided Tour (2018)

God, Hitler, and Lord Peter Wimsey: Selected Essays, Speeches and Articles by Dorothy L Sayers (2019)

Perth & Kinross: A Pocket Miscellany: A Companion for Visitors and Residents (2019)

The Piper of Tobruk: Pipe Major Robert Roy, MBE, DCM (2019)

The 'Gig Docter o Athole': Dr William Irvine & The Irvine Memorial Hospital (2019)

Afore the Highlands: The Jacobites in Perth, 1715–16 (2019)

'Where Sky and Summit Meet': Flight Over Perthshire – A History: Tales of Pilots, Airfields, Aeronautical Feats, & War (2019)

Diverted Traffic (2020)

Authentic Democracy: An Ethical Justification of Anarchism (2020)

'If Rivers Could Sing': A Scottish River Wildlife Journey. A Year in the Life of the River Devon as it flows through the Counties of Perthshire, Kinross-shire & Clackmannanshire (2020)

Shortlisted Scotland's National Book Awards 2021, 'New Book' (Saltire Literary Awards)

A Squatter o Bairnrhymes (2020)
by Stuart A Paterson, Scots Writer of the Year 2020

In a Sma Room Songbook: From the Poems by William Soutar (2020)

The Nicht Afore Christmas: the much-loved yuletide tale in Scots (2020)
Shortlisted for Scots Children's Book of the Year 2021

Ice Cold Blood (David Millar, 2021)

The Black Watch and the Great War
(Derek Patrick and Fraser Brown (editors), 2021)

The Perth Riverside Nursery & Beyond:
A Spirit of Enterprise and Improvement
(Elspeth Bruce and Pat Kerr, 2021)

Beyond the Swelkie: A Collection of Poems & Writings to Mark the Centenary of George Mackay Brown (1921-1996)
(Jim Mackintosh and Paul S Philippou (editors), 2021)

Dying to Live: The Remarkable True Story of Scotland's Sickest Survivor of Covid-19
(Grant and Amanda Macintyre, 2021)

The Shanter Legacy: The Search for the Grey Mare's Tail
(Garry Stewart, 2021)

Fatal Duty: Scotland's Cop Killers, Killer Cops & More... from 1812 to 1952 (Gary Knight, 2021)

A Scottish Wildlife Odyssey: In Search of Scotland's Wild Secrets (Keith Broomfield, 2022)

Sweet F.A.
(Tim Barrow, Paul Beeson and Bruce Strachan, 2022)

Forthcoming

William Soutar: Collected Poetry, Volume I
(Kirsteen McCue, Philippa Osmond-Williams and
Paul S Philippou (editors), 2022)

William Soutar: Collected Poetry, Volume II
(Kirsteen McCue, Philippa Osmond-Williams and
Paul S Philippou (editors), 2023)

Berries Fae Banes: An owersettin in Scots o the poems bi Pino Mereu scrievit in tribute tae Hamish Henderson
(Jim Macintosh, 2022)

Perthshire 101: A Poetic Gazetteer of the Big County
(Andy Jackson (editor), 2022)

Perth City Activity Book: Exploring the Past and Present
(Felicity Graham, 2022)

The Whole Damn Town (Hannah Ballantyne, 2022)

In the Shadow of Piper Alpha (Iain Maloney, 2022)

Balkan Rhapsody (Maria Kassimova-Moisset, translated by Iliyana Nedkova-Byrne, 2022)

All Tippermuir Books titles are available from bookshops and online booksellers. They can also be purchased directly (with free postage & packing (UK only) - minimum charges for overseas delivery) from **www.tippermuirbooks.co.uk.**

Tippermuir Books Ltd can be contacted at **mail@tippermuirbooks.co.uk.**